6
MINUTE
MORNING
TONING

6
MINUTE
MORNING
TONING

FAYE ROWE

Bath · New York · Singapore · Hong Kong · Cologne · Delhi · Melbourne

This edition published by Parragon in 2009

Parragon
Queen Street House
4 Queen Street
Bath BA1 1HE, UK

ISBN: 978-1-4075-8737-0

Printed in Malaysia

Produced by Ivy Contract
Photography: Ian Parsons
Model: Samantha Fuery
Exercise consultants: Dax Moy Personal Training Studios

The views expressed in this book are those of the author, but they are general views only,
and readers are urged to consult a relevant and qualified specialist for individual advice in
particular situations. Parragon hereby excludes all liability to the extent permitted by law
for any errors or omissions in this book and for any loss, damage, or expense (whether
direct or indirect) suffered by a third party relying on any information contained in this
book.

Ivy Contract would like to thank Jupiterimages Corporation for
permission to reproduce copyright material on pages 7 and 9.

Caution
Please check with your doctor/therapist before attempting this workout, particularly if you
have an injury, are pregnant, or have just had a baby. It is recommended that new mothers
wait at least six weeks postpartum before participating in exercise (12 weeks if it was a
Cesarean birth). If you feel any pain or discomfort at any point, please stop exercising
immediately and seek medical advice.

CONTENTS

INTRODUCTION

Making time for exercise in the morning is a great way to start the day. Not only will the toning exercises in this book help to put a spring in your step, but they'll also fire up your metabolism, so you'll burn more calories over the course of the day. Plus, a healthy dose of exercise will help to boost a sluggish circulatory system and leave your skin glowing and gorgeous.

Tone up in two weeks

Each of the exercises in this book has been chosen specifically to give you maximum results. So, even if you struggle to find time in the mornings, by making a concerted effort to set aside just six minutes every day, you'll find that you can achieve noticeable results within two weeks of sticking to the plan.

The best thing about this book is that it's aimed at everyone—even beginners. Even if you've never even set foot in a gym, you'll find the exercises easy to follow and fun to do.

Healthy living

After the two weeks are up, you may find that your clothes start to feel looser and that your muscles start to look more defined. Some people take a little longer to respond to exercise for a whole range of reasons, such as body composition—whether you naturally have more muscle mass—or other lifestyle factors.

While this book is a brilliant resource, it may also be worth considering making positive

changes to your lifestyle to help you along the way and maximize your results, especially if you're looking for a quick fix because you need to look great for a special occasion. Embarking on a healthy eating program is the perfect partner to a more active lifestyle—but remember, always speak to your doctor or a nutritionist before you make changes to your diet.

Simply making healthy food choices—cutting down on fat and sugar, eating lots of fresh fruit and vegetables, and drinking eight glasses (eight-and-a-half cups) of water a day—will help to flush toxins out of your system and make the body a more efficient machine so your muscles respond better to exercising. But even without the extra effort, you will slowly start to see your body become more toned and fit-looking. You may just have to repeat the two-week plan until you get the results you crave.

Once you've got used to the routine, it will become second nature and, hopefully, an enjoyable part of your life. Many studies have shown that exercise can be addictive, due to the rush of feel-good chemicals—serotonin and dopamine—that are released in the brain when you work out. It's exactly like eating chocolate, with none of the guilt!

The exercises

The exercises in this book have been chosen to help you tone up all over, so you'll get balanced results. They are divided into five different sections, which each target a specific part of the body. If you have a quick flick through, you'll find sections devoted to targeting legs, buttocks, tums and arms, in addition to a combined chest and back section. Some parts of the body, such as buttocks and thighs, are harder to tone, which is why you'll find more exercises for them.

Every exercise is carefully explained with step-by-step instructions and we've cut down on medical jargon so you know exactly which muscles you are targeting and where you should feel it working because—let's face it—we're not all experts on fitness.

Some exercises work your core muscles, such as those found deep within the torso. In turn, this helps to develop your core stability, which will help to prevent injury during exercise and correct your posture.

Exercises that work your core stability, such as the Superman on page 15, require you to "engage" your stomach muscles. You can do this by pulling in your tummy muscles toward your spine, being careful not to hold your breath. This should automatically cause you to straighten your posture and create the perfect starting position to carry out the exercise.

Before starting the plan you should seek advice from your doctor, especially if you are pregnant or suffer from back pain, in order to rule out any reason why it wouldn't be suitable for you.

Most of the exercises in this book are easy to do. If you do find any exercises particularly difficult to carry out, then you should stop attempting to do them and seek advice from a qualified fitness expert before carrying on. The most important thing to remember is that it's better to work within your comfort zone, rather than push yourself too hard. It's also important to remember that even when an exercise requires you to fully extend your arms or legs, you must not lock your elbows or knees in order to help guard against injury.

Practice makes perfect

Before you start the two-week plan, take time to familiarize yourself with the different exercises. Perhaps spend a few hours one afternoon going through the poses to make sure you're confident that you're doing them correctly. Practice each exercise a few times so it's clear in your head how each one is supposed to feel. You should also get into the habit of setting a stopwatch on your wrist or keeping an alarm clock close to hand so you can accurately time how long it takes you to do each exercise. Your aim is to do each of the exercises for 30 seconds. Usually, to make the exercise last for that amount of time you will need to do a certain number of repetitions (known as reps, which is the term we've adopted in this book). Again, we've given an indication of how many reps you should try to achieve for each exercise, but you should always go at your own pace. As long as you complete the six-minute routine, without pausing for more than a couple of seconds at a time, you will have done enough to yield results.

An important thing to remember is that you should never feel any pain while doing any of the exercises. In the unlikely event that you do feel pain, or an exercise simply doesn't feel right, you should stop doing

the exercise immediately and seek advice from your doctor to help rule out any underlying medical condition that could be causing it.

Warming up

To help guard against injury and make your body as receptive to the exercises as possible, we've included a one-minute warm-up plan at the start of the book. Make sure you always start with the warm-up before moving on to the six-minute exercise routine.

If you look at the two-week plan (see page 44), you'll see clearly how to fit the

warm-up and the exercises into six minutes. We've made it easy for you to see what you should be doing on which day. By combining exercises from each section, it will help you to target the body as a whole and stop you from overworking one specific area. However, if you want to target a particular problem zone, you have the option to tailor the plan to suit by adding more exercises from that section to your routine.

What you need

All the exercises in this book have been devised so that you need minimal equipment. However, there are some basic things you need to get your hands on before you start:

- A well-made pair of sneakers, which will support your feet. Most sports stores now have a great range and will be able to advise you about choosing the best pair to suit the type of exercise you are doing.
- A pair of jogging pants or shorts, a breathable T-shirt or sleeveless top, and a sports bra, will allow you to move easily and do all the exercises to the best of your ability.
- You could invest in a padded exercise mat, which can be found in most sports stores and even some supermarkets.
- You may choose to invest in a set of dumbbells, which can be bought from most sports stores. Choose a weight that's challenging, but not impossible to work with—the store staff will be able to advise you.

Two weeks to a better body

When the two weeks are up, one of the biggest changes you will notice in yourself is in performance. It depends how fit you already are when you start this program, but you should definitely be able to increase the number of reps you can manage of each exercise during the 30 seconds of allotted time.

If you aren't used to exercising, doing six minutes a day for two weeks adds up to a fair bit and you will notice more dramatic effects, such as weight loss and firmer, more toned muscles.

If you find that you're struggling to make time for exercise in the mornings, try these top tips:

- Visualize how your body will look and how you will feel if you stick religiously to the plan. It will help you to realize why doing the exercises every morning is essential.
- Try setting your alarm half an hour earlier than you usually do—you can have an extra 10-minute sleep and still have time to exercise.
- Invest in some flattering sportswear—it will make you want to jump out of bed just to wear it.
- Start the day with a cup of warm water and a slice of lemon—it will help to detox your system and focus your mind.
- You could try playing some upbeat, motivating music while you do the routine.

Getting started

To get started, use the example two-week planner at the back of the book to guide you. If you want to develop your own two-week plan later, you can do. It's recommended that, on top of warming up, you choose six of the 30-second exercises and repeat them, so you are exercising for six minutes in total.

You can see from our guide that we've chosen a good mix of exercises to work each different body part, so if you want to make your own plan, be sure to keep this in mind. All you have to do now is get motivated, get ready, and get moving!

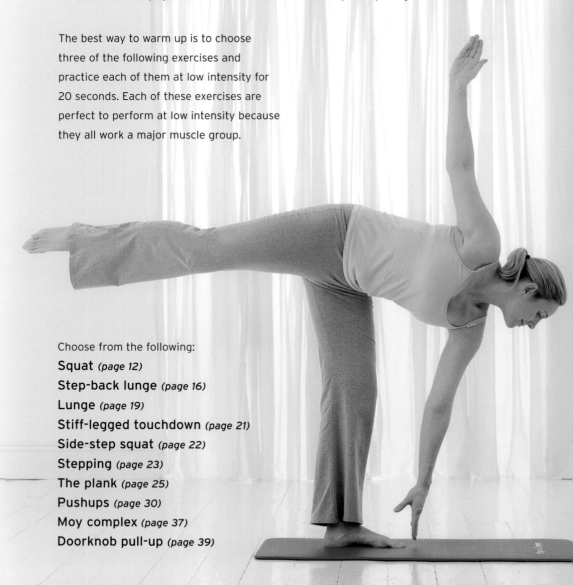

ONE-MINUTE WARM-UP

Before you do any kind of exercise, it's important to spend time warming up so that your muscles are primed and ready to work. Not only will the warm-up help prevent you from straining any muscles, but it will also help you to work more efficiently, so you get better results.

The best way to warm up is to choose three of the following exercises and practice each of them at low intensity for 20 seconds. Each of these exercises are perfect to perform at low intensity because they all work a major muscle group.

Choose from the following:

Squat *(page 12)*
Step-back lunge *(page 16)*
Lunge *(page 19)*
Stiff-legged touchdown *(page 21)*
Side-step squat *(page 22)*
Stepping *(page 23)*
The plank *(page 25)*
Pushups *(page 30)*
Moy complex *(page 37)*
Doorknob pull-up *(page 39)*

Once you've picked your three exercises, run through each one slowly, at a controlled pace, for 20 seconds each. You should be able to manage around five to eight repetitions of each exercise.

Don't try to rush—remember that the warm-up is there to make sure your muscles are, literally, warm and ready for exercise.

Try to swap around your choice of warm-up exercises each day, like we've done in the two-week planner, so you keep the routine fresh and exciting to do.

Once you've completed the minute-long sequence, turn to your planner and go straight into the main exercise regime.

Squat

The Squat is one of the most effective exercises for toning the muscles in the legs and buttocks, including the hamstrings (at the back of the legs). Plus, it's a great way to build strength in the lower body. It's an easy exercise to get right and you can really feel it working.

1 Stand with feet hip-width apart. You can either place your hands on your hips or hold on to the back of a chair for support if needed.

2 Look straight ahead and count to three while you bend your knees and push your bottom out behind you, until you feel the muscles working in the backs of your thighs and buttocks. The deeper you can squat, the better it is for working those muscles, but make sure you keep your feet flat on the floor at all times. Keep your back straight and make sure your spine is in line with your head and neck.

3 Return to the starting position, counting to three as you go, then get ready to do it all over again.

Number of reps: Aim for around 10.

2

WATCH POINT
Make sure your feet remain flat on the floor. Don't let them rise up when you bend your knees.

Lying hip rotations

This exercise tones and strengthens the muscles in the hips, so is great for improving the appearance of the dreaded saddlebags (those annoying pockets of fat that can appear on the outside of the top of the thighs). By clenching your buttocks as you rotate your hip, you'll be giving them a workout too.

1 Lie on your left side, bending your left knee so it's at a 45-degree angle to your body.

2 Lift up and support your upper body with your left hand and arm—this should be a comfortable resting position. Place your right hand on the floor in front of you for additional support.

3 Contract your buttocks and raise your right leg off the floor from the hip joint as far as you can toward the ceiling, keeping the foot flexed (and bent at the ankle).

WATCH POINT
Try to get your leg as high as you can without straining—you'll find it gets easier with practice.

3

4 Gently lower your leg out in front of you, down toward the floor so it's at a right angle to your body. Keep it as straight as you can without locking your knee.

5 Bring your right leg back into the starting position, keeping it just off the floor.

Number of reps: Do three or more reps on one side and then reverse the entire movement and do the same on the other side.

4

Standing calf raises

The calf muscles are hard to target, although studies have shown that walking in high heels can help to tone them up! To get really sexy, shapely calves, we recommend you try this exercise instead.

2

1 Stand with both feet near the edge of a raised object such as a stair or a big chunky book. Place the ball of your right foot on the edge of the raised object, letting your heel extend off the edge.

2 Hold on to a wall or a chair for support and, lifting your left leg into the air slightly by bending at the knee, gently let your right heel drop down until you feel the stretch in your calf. Keep your back straight, your head up, and your right leg straight.

3 Rise up onto your right toe as high as you can and hold for a second while flexing the calf muscle.

4 Carefully return to the starting position, then repeat with the left leg.

Number of reps: Aim to do around 10 on each foot.

WATCH POINT
Make sure that you don't slip off the raised object by carefully controlling the move. If that means you have to do fewer than 10 reps on each foot during the 30 seconds, so be it.

Superman

You need to have a good sense of balance to do this exercise, so if you don't get it right first time, be patient. It's great for increasing core stability and endurance in the joints, as well as working the core muscles in your thighs.

1 Get down on the floor on all fours.

2 Contract your abs. Extend your right arm out in front of you and your left leg out behind you, keeping them as straight as you can without locking your elbow or knee. Engage your abdominal muscles to help stop your back from arching—it will reduce any risk of injury. You will feel the muscles working in the thigh of your extended leg. To increase the effects, try pointing your toes—it will make you tense your muscles harder. Keep your head and neck in line with your back to make sure you're not twisting your neck.

3 Slowly return to the start position and repeat with the opposite leg and arm.

Number of reps: Beginners should hold the position for 12 seconds then swap, but if you feel comfortable, try moving your arm and leg in and out for extra toning effects.

WATCH POINT
Do this on soft carpet or a padded exercise mat,
so you don't hurt your knees.

Step-back lunge

This exercise will help to tone the quadriceps (known as the quad muscles) at the front of your thighs to give you a healthy and athletic look.

1 Stand with feet hip-width apart and rest your hands on your hips.

2 Keep your right foot firmly on the floor and lunge backward with your left leg, bending your knee until it rests around six inches above the floor. You should be balancing on the ball of your left foot, and will be able to feel the muscles working in the front of the left thigh.

3 Return to the starting position, then repeat with the other leg.

Number of reps: Aim to do around three on each leg, or more if you feel comfortable.

WATCH POINT

Check behind you to make sure you have enough room to step back into the lunge. If you want to make the exercise more demanding, you can hold dumbbells as you do it.

1

2

Sidekick

The Sidekick is an energetic exercise that will get your heart rate pumping and really burn some calories. It's great for toning the hamstrings and quads and it will give your waist a workout too.

1 Stand with feet hip-width apart. Bring your hands up to your chest and form loose fists, while keeping your elbows bent and by your sides to help you balance.

2 Raise your right leg off the floor and kick it out to the side in a swift, controlled move. Be careful not to flick your leg, as you could jar your knee or hip.

3 Bring your leg back to the starting position and repeat the movement for 30 seconds.

4 Repeat the movement with your left leg.

Number of reps: Aim to do around 10 on each leg.

1

2

WATCH POINT
Be careful that you don't use too much force to shoot your leg out to the side or you may end up straining a muscle or jarring your knee.

Rear leg raise

This exercise will help to strengthen and tone both the gluteus maximus (the major muscles in the buttocks, which are also known as the glutes) and also the lower back.

1 Lie face-down on the floor with your forehead resting on the backs of your hands. Make sure your spine is in line with your neck.

2 Squeeze your buttocks—it will make the exercise more effective. Then, engage your abdominal muscles and gently lift your right leg off the floor until you feel the muscles working in your buttocks. Keep your leg straight and your knee soft. You shouldn't feel any pain in your lower back.

3 Lower your right leg back into the starting position then repeat the movement with your left leg and again with your right, and so on until the 30 seconds are up.

Number of reps: Aim to complete around three sets of 10 reps. You can do five sets of six with a slight pause between if you prefer.

WATCH POINT
Don't try to lift your leg too high or it will force your back to arch and put a strain on the muscles.

Lunge

This is different from the Step-back lunge, which works the muscles in the legs, because shifting your core body weight to the front means that the muscles in your buttocks will bear most of the brunt. Lunging is great for strengthening as well as toning the muscles and is a firm favorite among personal fitness trainers.

1 Stand with your feet hip-width apart. Rest your hands on your hips or by your sides.

2 Step forward with your right leg, bending your knee so your thigh is almost at a right angle to the floor. Your right foot should be flat on the floor. Your left leg should be slightly bent at the knee and the ball of your left foot should be resting on the floor behind you, with your heel slightly in the air.

3 Hold for a second, then push off the floor with your right foot and return to the starting position.

4 Repeat the movement with alternate legs until the 30 seconds are up.

Number of reps: Aim to do around 10 lunges (five on each side) in the allotted time.

WATCH POINT
Don't rush the lunge or go down too far or you'll end up banging your knee on the floor. Always make sure you go at your own pace.

2

Crane stand

This exercise is like the Superman, but standing up. It's great for working your buttocks, hamstrings, and lower back but it does take a lot of skill and balance to achieve, so do it slowly for best results.

1 Stand on your left leg and take a few seconds to find your balance.

2 Extend your left arm out in front of you and your right leg out behind you. Try to keep your right leg as straight as possible without locking the knee.

3 Reach out as far as possible and tilt your body over from the waist so your left arm drops down to the floor.

4 Gently straighten up from the waist so you're back in the starting position.

5 Repeat with the opposite arm and leg.

2

3

Number of reps: Aim to do around four, or more if you feel comfortable.

WATCH POINT
This exercise is suitable for everyone. Just concentrate and take it slowly to make sure you keep your balance.

Stiff-legged touchdown

This exercise takes a bit of skill and balance to execute, but the results are worth it. Stretching down to touch your toes from a standing position will work all the supporting muscles around your buttocks and thighs and help improve your core stability. It's similar to the Crane stand, but you are bending from the waist.

1 Stand with feet hip-width apart. Rest your hands on your hips or by your side. Lift your right leg off the floor and take a second to find your balance. You may need to rest the tips of your toes on the floor if you feel you are about to topple over.

2 Reach down and try to touch the toes of your "stiff" (straight) left leg with your left arm. Make sure that you keep your left leg straight and your knee soft.

3 At the same time, extend your right leg backwards (don't lock the knee). Raise your right arm for balance. If you can't reach your toes, allow your hand to hover in the air as far down as is comfortable.

4 Slowly return to the starting position and repeat with the other leg.

Number of reps: Hold the pose for around 10 seconds, then repeat with the other leg.

Side-step squat

This exercise is an 80s aerobics classic, which is so effective that it's still used today in most good fitness routines. Squatting to the side targets all the muscles along the inner thigh and bottom to help sculpt a beautiful-looking rear view.

1 Stand feet hip-width apart, with your feet slightly turned out and flat on the floor. Rest your hands on your hips or by your sides.

2 Step your right leg out to the side and bend your right knee, so you lower yourself by a few inches down toward the floor. Let your full body weight fall onto your right leg. Keep both feet firmly on the floor at all times.

3 Push off from the floor with your right foot and return to the starting position.

4 Repeat the movement with your left leg and keep repeating the exercise on alternate legs until the 30 seconds are up.

Number of reps: Aim to do around 10 Side-step squats on each leg.

1

2

WATCH POINT
Doing the full warm-up routine at the start of this book will help you avoid pulling the muscles in your groin as you do this exercise.

FOR THE BOTTOM

Stepping

This is a great exercise if you like "feeling the burn." Stepping up onto a stair forces the glutes (the muscles in the buttocks) to squeeze and contract, so will help create a pert bottom.

1 Stand at the bottom of the stairs or in front of a big chunky book. Rest your hands on your hips or let them rest by your sides.

2 Step up onto the step with your left leg and let your right leg follow.

3 Step down off the step with your left leg and let the right leg follow.

4 Repeat, starting with the right leg.

Number of reps: You should be able to manage around 15 or more during the 30 seconds.

WATCH POINT
If you choose to wear something on your feet, wear a good pair of sports sneakers rather than slippery socks for this exercise so that you don't slip off the step. Plus, don't rush the move.

Reverse curl

This is great for targeting the stomach muscles. You should feel it really working all across your tummy—the harder you concentrate, the more effective it will be.

1 Lie on the floor, making sure that the small of your back is pressed against the floor and not arching upward. An easy way to do this is to engage your abdominal muscles so you feel them contract.

2 Bring your knees toward your chest and cross your feet at the ankles. Rest your hands by your sides on the floor for support.

3 In one carefully controlled move, use your stomach muscles to lift your bottom and lower back off the floor. Aim to straighten your feet and knees and push them up toward the ceiling. You don't have to move far, just enough to feel your muscles working.

4 Count to two on the way up and two on the way down.

5 When you've done 30 seconds' worth of reps, place your feet back on the floor. Return to your starting position.

Number of reps: Aim to do around seven reps during the 30 seconds.

WATCH POINT

Make sure you're lying on soft carpet or a padded exercise mat to reduce the risk of bruising your spine. If you're a complete beginner, a slightly easier version of the Reverse curl is to use your stomach muscles to bring your knees further in toward your chest rather than up toward the ceiling.

The plank

This doesn't sound or look too taxing but, if you do it right, you'll find that it's one of the most intense exercises in the book, and very effective for toning the abdominal muscles. Many people, especially beginners, find this difficult to hold for long periods of time, so see how you get on. Aim to hold for the full 30 seconds by the end of two weeks.

1 Lie on the floor on your front, resting your forehead on the backs of your hands.

2 Keeping your elbows bent, slide your hands across the floor, rotating from the shoulders, until you find your perfect "pushup" position at either side of your chest.

3 Curl your toes underneath you and push up off the floor with your hands. Keep your elbows soft to stop them locking, and keep your neck and head relaxed and in line with your spine.

4 Hold the pose for 10 seconds, then gently lower yourself back down to the floor again. Remember to breathe during the exercise.

Number of reps: Start by doing three sets of 10 seconds and try to increase the time that you hold the Plank to the full 30 seconds by the end of two weeks.

WATCH POINT
This exercise can be difficult to do so don't overstrain yourself—you may be able to hold the position for only five seconds at first. Just persevere!

FOR THE STOMACH

2

Stomach tuck-in

This exercise is like the natural alternative to wearing a corset. It works the deep muscles in your stomach—the transverse abdominals—to help flatten and define the muscles in your tum. It's the perfect start to getting a super-flat stomach.

1 Stand with feet hip-width apart and hands resting by your sides.

2 Slowly contract your abs (your stomach muscles) by pulling them in toward your spine, but don't hold your breath. If you put your hand on your tummy you should feel the muscles tighten—this means they're working. For best results, really concentrate on what you're doing and how it feels.

3 Slowly release and get ready to start again.

Number of reps: Hold for 10 seconds and repeat three times.

WATCH POINT
This exercise can also be done sitting on a chair.

Waist twist

Make sure you have a lot of space around you so that when you swing your arms you don't hit anything. This is a fun exercise to do and it really gets to work on the obliques (the muscles at the side of your waist), to help define a curvy silhouette.

1 Stand with feet hip-width apart, hands by sides, and knees slightly bent.

2 Extend your arms out in front of you and form loose fists with your hands.

3 Swing your arms from side to side, making sure your feet stay firmly on the floor and your hips face forward. Start off slowly and then build up speed, making sure you keep control of the movement and your hips stay facing the front.

4 When the 30 seconds are up, drop your arms back down by your sides, and return to the starting position.

Number of reps: Do as many as you can in the 30 seconds.

WATCH POINT
Don't get carried away while swinging your arms because you may end up pulling a muscle. If you have to go slowly to control the movement, so be it.

3

Crunches

This is an intense workout for your stomach muscles and a great way of getting a washboard-flat tum.

1 Lie on the floor, with your knees bent and feet (apart) flat on the floor in line with your hips. Make sure your lower back is pressed into the floor. Put your hands behind your head to support your neck.

2 Engage your stomach muscles, by pulling your abs toward your spine, and lift your upper body off the floor as far as you can without arching your lower back. You may find that you can't get up very high, but it's the effort of moving that counts, so make sure that you're pushing yourself as hard as you comfortably can. With practice, you may be able to sit up completely.

3 When you can't go any further, pause for one second. Then gently lower yourself back down into the starting position and repeat.

Number of reps: Try to do as many sets of five as possible, with a brief rest between. By the end of two weeks you should aim to do the Crunches continuously for 30 seconds.

WATCH POINT
Make sure you don't use your neck to pull yourself up or you'll feel the strain the next day. Supporting your neck with your hands will prevent this, but don't use your hands to lift your head off the floor— let your tummy muscles do all the work.

1

3

FOR THE STOMACH

The bicycle

This is similar to the Crunches exercise, but crossing your elbow to the opposite knee targets the obliques instead, which are found at the side of the waist. Practicing this exercise will help give you a smaller, more defined middle.

1 Lie on the floor with your knees bent and feet flat on the floor.

2 Rest your hands behind your head and, using your stomach muscles, lift your upper body off the floor, making sure that your lower back stays firmly on the floor.

3 Lift your right foot off the floor and bring your right knee toward your chest.

4 Reach forward and rotate from the waist slightly in order to bring your left elbow toward your right knee. They don't have to touch.

5 Pause for one second then return to the starting position. Repeat the movement, bringing your right elbow toward your left knee.

6 Continue the exercise on alternate sides until the 30 seconds are up.

Number of reps: Aim to do as many as you can in the 30 seconds—around 12. Take a brief pause if you have to—for example, between sets of six.

WATCH POINT
Make sure your head and neck are in line with your spine and that you're looking up toward the ceiling—it will prevent you from straining your neck.

3

4

Pushups

This is a good all-round exercise for toning the major muscles in the arms. It's really good for developing upper-body strength and balancing out a pear-shaped figure.

1 Lie face-down on the floor, with your forehead resting on the backs of your hands. Slide your hands around to rest at shoulder level, to find your ideal "pushup" position either side of your chest.

2 Use your arms to lift your upper body off the floor and bring your knees in toward your chest a little so they're resting on the floor, taking most of your body weight. Cross your feet at the ankles and raise them off the floor slightly. This should automatically cause your body weight to shift back onto your arms.

3 Bend your elbows and gently lower your upper body back down to the floor, keeping your head and shoulders level and in line with your spine at all times. Then push off the floor with your hands, raising your upper body into the air. Aim to get your arms straight, while keeping your elbows soft. Repeat this movement.

Number of reps: Aim for two sets of 10 during the 30 seconds.

WATCH POINT

Engaging your tummy muscles will help keep your back straight and reduce any risk of injury. When the Pushups become easier to do, extend your legs fully out behind you and curl your toes under so they remain on the floor instead of your knees when you push up.

2

3

FOR THE ARMS

Bicep curl

The biceps are the muscles at the front of the upper arms. They are relatively easy to tone, so practicing this exercise will help give you shapely arms that you'll want to show off.

1 Stand up tall with feet hip-width apart and knees soft.

2 Extend your arms out in front of you with palms facing upward, holding a can of soup or a dumbbell in each hand.

3 Bend your elbows and bring both your hands in toward you so that your arms form right angles.

4 Reverse the movement so that your elbows are fully extended in front of you again. Keep your elbows soft at all times.

5 Repeat the movement until the 30 seconds are up.

Number of reps: Aim to do as many as you can during the time period without rushing.

WATCH POINT
Read the guidelines for choosing dumbbells in the introduction of this book, so you're working with the right weight for you.

Tricep extension

The triceps are the muscles at the back of the upper arms. If they're left to slack, it can lead to the dreaded "bingo wing" effect, where loose skin on the underside of your arms wobbles as you wave. It's classically a hard muscle to target, but this exercise will help to tighten and tone.

1 Stand with feet hip-width apart. Pick up a heavy object with both hands—choose something that you can work comfortably with, such as a dumbbell or a heavy book.

2 Bring the object over your head with straight arms.

3 Bend your arms at the elbows, so you slowly lower it down between your shoulder blades.

4 Reverse the movement by straightening your arms so you bring the object directly back above your head.

5 Repeat Steps 3 and 4 slowly, so you're in control of the movement.

Number of reps: Aim to do around seven reps in the 30 seconds.

WATCH POINT
Choose a weight that's challenging but not so heavy that you can't control it—you don't want to end up dropping it on your head.

3

4

Bench dip

As well as working your triceps, this will help improve your core stability and tone up your tummy. It's especially great for the arms because you're using your body weight to strengthen and tone.

1 Sit on the edge of a chair with your hands resting either side of your bottom, gripping the edge of the seat.

2 Walk your feet away from the chair as far as you can so your bottom comes off the edge of the chair.

3 Letting your arms take your body weight, bend your elbows and, with knees bent, slowly lower your body toward the floor—make sure you don't end up sitting on the floor; hovering just above the floor is the ideal position. Make sure your weight is evenly distributed so you don't topple the chair.

4 Straighten your arms, so you bring your lower body back up. Repeat Steps 3 and 4.

Number of reps: Aim for around six reps.

WATCH POINT
Keep your forearms vertical at all times—it will help to reduce the amount of strain on your shoulders.

Tricep kickback

This is another great exercise that will help to banish "bingo wings" and tone up those hard-to-target tricep muscles at the back of the upper arms. When you do this exercise, make sure that your arm extends directly out behind you rather than veering off to the side.

1

3 Bend your left elbow and bring the dumbbell back to the start position, next to your shoulder.

4 Repeat around 12 times and then swap your position so you're doing the exercise with the right arm.

Number of reps: Do around 10-12 with one arm, then swap to work the other.

WATCH POINT
Be careful not to swing your arm while doing the movement—you'll get better results if you do it more slowly and stay in control.

2

1 Grab yourself a chair and rest your right hand and right knee on the seat. Keep your left leg straight with your knee soft and hold a dumbbell or can of soup in your left hand.

2 Bend your left elbow and bring your left hand up to shoulder height, then "kickback" with your left arm so it's fully extended out behind you. Although we call it a kickback, you should carry out the movement in a slow and controlled manner.

Circles in the air

This exercise is great for general toning of the arms and shoulders. Using weights will also help to develop strength in the arms and have a pumping effect on the muscles, so you'll look great in short-sleeved tops.

1 Stand with feet hip-width apart, knees slightly bent, and arms resting by your sides.

2 With a dumbbell in each hand, cross your arms in front of each other level with your hips, then circle them up toward the ceiling so they cross over in the air above your head. Then bring them back round to the starting position.

3 Pause for one second then repeat the movement in the opposite direction.

Number of reps: Aim to do around 15 in the 30 seconds.

WATCH POINT
Keep your arms fully extended as you circle them so you are working as many muscles as possible, but remember to keep your elbows soft.

Reverse sit-up

This is a great exercise for strengthening the lower back. Adding an arm rotation to the move delivers a double toning boost to the shoulders.

1 Lie face-down on the floor with your forehead resting on the backs of your hands.

2 Squeeze your buttocks and use your stomach muscles to raise your chest off the floor as far as you feel comfortable.

1

3 Squeeze your shoulder blades together by rotating your arms around from the shoulders so your palms are facing downward and your forearms are hovering at chest level. This will help to give the shoulders a workout, too.

4 Return your arms to the starting position and lower your chest back down to the floor. Repeat the movement.

Number of reps: Aim to do around 15 or more during the 30 seconds.

WATCH POINT

Don't try to pull your chest back too far or it will force your lower back to arch and put a strain on the muscles. Just do what feels comfortable.

3

Moy complex

This exercise is also known as the "row, rotate, and press" and is a great way to tone the muscles in your back, without having to use the complicated machinery that you find in the gym.

1 Sit on the edge of a chair with a dumbbell or can of soup in each hand.

2 Bend over from the waist so your chest is resting on your knees. Make sure your head and neck are relaxed, so that you're looking down toward the floor.

3 Start with your hands resting on the floor, with elbows slightly bent, then bend your arms and bring your hands up to shoulder level.

4 Rotate your wrists and extend your arms out in front of you so that they're parallel to the floor.

5 Retrace your steps so you're back in the Step 2 position, then repeat the movement.

Number of reps: Aim to do around 15 reps during the 30 seconds.

WATCH POINT
Remember to relax your head and neck and keep them in line with your spine, so you don't strain any muscles.

Dumbbell row

Doing this exercise is like starting a lawn mower. It targets the muscles in the middle of the back, such as the trapezius. So, if you practice this religiously, it will make wearing backless dresses all the more appealing.

1 Rest your right knee and your right hand on the seat of a chair, like you do for the Tricep kickback.

2 Holding a dumbbell or can of soup in your left hand, pull it back toward your hip.

3 Extend your left arm diagonally out in front of you, so that it travels toward the ground.

4 Bring the dumbbell back to your hip and repeat the movement.

Number of reps: Aim to do around 10–12 on your left arm before swapping your position so you're working your right arm for the remainder of the 30 seconds.

WATCH POINT
You should do this exercise on one side at a time if you have a bad back. If you want to work both sides at once, take away the chair and stand in a squat position while doing the exercise.

2

3

Doorknob pull-up

It sounds strange, but this is a perfect exercise to do at home. As you lean back, the resistance created by holding the towel around the doorknobs will give all the muscles in your back a good workout.

1 Open a suitable door and wrap a hand towel around the doorknobs.

2 Making sure it's secure, drop down into a squat position, holding one end of the towel in each hand. You should be leaning back from the waist, taking the slack from the towel so you feel the muscles working in your back.

WATCH POINT
Don't rush this exercise. You'll feel a greater resistance if you do it slowly and carefully rather than trying to fit as many as possible into the 30 seconds.

3 Hold for a few seconds then pull yourself back up to a standing position and repeat the movement.

Number of reps: Try to do around 20 in the 30 seconds.

3

Wall pushup

This is like a standing pushup and is great for toning the muscles in the chest, especially the pectoral muscles (known as the pecs), which can be found underneath your bust. If you master the move, it will help you to achieve a perky bust without having to resort to surgery!

WATCH POINT
Make sure you really put some effort into pushing off from the wall—that way it will work your arms as well as your chest.

1 Stand around 2 feet (60 cm) away from the wall, feet hip-width apart and legs straight. Make sure your knees are soft.

2 Lean forward and place your palms flat against the wall.

3 Bend your arms at the elbows and bring your chest toward the wall.

4 Squeeze the muscles in your chest and push off from the wall so you are standing back in the start position.

Number of reps: Aim for around 15 reps during the 30 seconds.

FOR CHEST & BACK

3

The prayer

This is excellent for toning the pectoral muscles (the pecs). Like the Wall pushup exercise, toning these muscles will help to give you a more youthful-looking bust.

1 Either while standing or sitting, press the palms of your hands together at shoulder height while extending your elbows out to the sides.

2 Hold the pose for as long as you can– ideally around 10 seconds–pressing your palms together with as much force as feels comfortable. Take one second to rest and then repeat the pose until the 30 seconds are up.

Number of reps: Aim to hold the pose for 10 seconds and then take one second to rest and start again. By the end of two weeks you should aim to hold the pose for the full 30 seconds.

WATCH POINT

Many people will find their joints crack when doing this exercise, so start by pressing the palms lightly together and gradually build up the pressure. Doing the exercise this way will help prevent you from getting cramp.

1

The fly

The weights used in this exercise will give the muscles in your chest an extra toning boost and help to build strength in the arms too. It's a great all-round upper body workout.

1 Lie on the floor on your back and hold a dumbbell or can of soup in each hand. Bend your knees and place your feet flat on the floor.

2 Extend both arms at a right angle to your body so that you're in a crucifix position.

3 Keeping your arms straight, with elbows soft, gently lift them above your head so that you bring the dumbbells together.

4 Pause for a second then gently lower arms back to the floor to the start position. Repeat.

Number of reps: Aim to do around three reps, then pause for a few seconds and repeat until the 30 seconds are up.

WATCH POINT
Make sure your arms are not bent—keep your elbows soft throughout the exercise.

4

3

Soup-can press

This exercise is great for toning the muscles in your chest and around your clavicle (collarbone) to help give you a slinky look. Make it a priority if you're aiming to squeeze into a strapless dress in two weeks.

1 Lie on your back, with your knees bent, and feet flat on the floor, holding a dumbbell or can of soup in each hand.

2 Bend your elbows and rest your hands by your armpits, so they're hovering just above your shoulders.

3 Extend your arms into the air at a right angle to your body, holding the dumbbells directly over your shoulders with your palms facing away from you.

4 Pull in your abdominals and tilt your chin in toward your chest.

5 Release your chin, then bend your elbows and bring your hands back to the starting position. Pause for one second then repeat.

Number of reps: Aim to do around 15 reps.

WATCH POINT
Push from the shoulders as your extend your arms, for maximum effects. Plus, make sure your lower back is pushed into the floor all the time you're doing this exercise.

2

3

TWO-WEEK PLAN

This two-week plan is an example of the way you can structure your exercise regime. We've chosen exercises to target each of the major muscle groups in the body to give you a great all-over workout.

Each morning you will start with a brief warm-up. We've picked six different exercises each day to create a three-minute routine, which should be carried out twice to make the workout last a total of six minutes.

You can easily draw up your own plan if you prefer. Make sure you include a good mix of exercises but, if you want to aim for weight loss as well as toning, remember that the standing exercises will burn a lot more calories than the others. Plus, any exercise that targets the legs is going to create a big calorie expenditure. Only you can know your body's major trouble zones, so can include extra exercises to target those particular areas.

We recommend you start with our plan and monitor your results. If you choose to do the two-week plan again at some point in the future, that's when you can adjust it if you wish. Now, lets get started.

Day 1

Squat **p12**
Sidekick **p17**
Rear leg raise **p18**
Reverse curl **p24**
Pushups **p30**
Reverse sit-up **p36**

Day 2

Lying hip rotations **p13**
Lunge **p19**
Stepping **p23**
The plank **p25**
Bicep curl **p31**
Moy complex **p37**

Day 3

Day 5

Day 4

Day 6

Day 7

Squat **p12**
Rear leg raise **p18**
Side-step squat **p22**
Reverse curl **p24**
Pushups **p30**
The fly **p42**

Day 9

Standing calf raises **p14**
Crane stand **p20**
Stomach tuck-in **p26**
Tricep extension **p32**
Tricep kickback **p34**
Reverse sit-up **p36**

Day 8

Lying hip rotations **p13**
Lunge **p19**
The plank **p25**
Crunches **p28**
Bicep curl **p31**
Soup-can press **p43**

Day 10

Superman **p15**
Stiff-legged touchdown **p21**
Waist twist **p27**
Bench dip **p33**
Moy complex **p37**
The fly **p42**

Day 11

Standing calf raises **p14**
Step-back lunge **p16**
Side-step squat **p22**
Crunches **p28**
Tricep kickback **p34**
Dumbbell row **p38**

Day 12

Step-back lunge **p16**
Stiff-legged touchdown **p21**
Side-step squat **p22**
Crunches **p28**
Tricep kickback **p34**
Dumbbell row **p38**

Day 13

Sidekick **p17**
Stepping **p23**
Waist twist **p27**
The bicycle **p29**
Circles in the air **p35**
Doorknob pull-up **p39**

Day 14

Squat **p12**
Rear leg raise **p18**
Reverse curl **p24**
Pushups **p30**
Bench dip **p33**
Wall pushup **p40**

INDEX